AMERICA'S MOST WANTED

Public Enemy Number One:
"MACHINE GUN" KELLY

Written by:
Sue L. Hamilton

Published by Abdo & Daughters, 6537 Cecilia Circle, Bloomington, Minnesota 55435

Library bound edition distributed by Rockbottom Books, Pentagon Tower, P.O. Box 36036, Minneapolis, Minnesota 55435

Library of Congress Number: 89-084924   ISBN: 0-939179-64-4

Cover Photos by: Bettmann Archive
Inside Photos by: Bettmann Archive

Edited by: John C. Hamilton

FORWARD

Saturday, July 22, 1933 11:15 p.m.

"Stick 'em up!" growled the 6'1" heavyset man as he flung open the screen door. The two couples playing cards on the porch stopped cold, a machine gun pointed directly at them. A second man stepped up and aimed his gun at the four startled people. "Which one's Urschel?" asked the big man.

No one spoke or moved. Charles Urschel, a millionaire oilman and one of the wealthiest people in Oklahoma, sat quietly, his cards still in hand. Beside him sat his wife and two friends, Mr. and Mrs. Walter Jarrett. Their card game lay forgotten as they faced the two men with guns.

"Well, which one is it?" repeated "Machine Gun" Kelly.

Urschel and Walter Jarrett remained silent. Jarrett was not going to give up his friend.

"All right," snarled Kelly, mad because neither he nor his partner, Albert Bates, had bothered to get a picture of Urschel to see what he looked like. "We'll take both of you."

Motioning with his machine gun, Kelly ordered the two men off the porch. "Don't call the police," he warned the two frightened women. His steely blue eyes glared coldly through the eerie darkness. The men moved away from the house, toward the kidnappers' waiting car.

After forcing the men into the Chevrolet sedan, they raced away. Just a few miles outside of Oklahoma City, Kelly had an idea. He stopped on a dark, empty road. "OK, empty your pockets," growled the big man. Kelly picked up the wallets and peered closely at their I.D.'s. Looking up, he said to Bates, "This one is Urschel. Toss the other guy out."

Bates opened the door and pulled Jarrett roughly to the ground. "So long," laughed Bates, getting back into the car. Kelly hit the gas, leaving Jarrett standing alone in the pitch black night.

As he watched his friend being driven away, Jarrett muttered to himself, "Good luck, Charlie."

4

Kidnappers' waiting car.

Turning, he stumbled down the road, heading back towards town.

In the car, Kelly was pleased. He knew his wife, Kathryn, was going to be happy. The kidnapping had been her idea. Now all they had to do was collect the $200,000 on this guy, and they could live a life of luxury. "We did it, Al," smiled Kelly, "We really did it."

"Yeah," replied Bates. "We'll be rich!"

In the back seat, tied and blindfolded, Charles Urschel sat listening carefully to every sound and movement inside and outside the car. He willed himself to remember everything — every stop, every turn, every smell. It was Urschel's brilliant memory that would take Machine Gun Kelly's first big-time job and turn it into the biggest mistake of his life.

CHAPTER 1 — KELLY AND KATHRYN

Machine Gun Kelly gained his reputation not through his own actions, but through stories made up by his wife. Born in 1897, the young

"George Kelly Barnes" grew up in Tennessee. His parents were not rich, but they got by. He had some schooling, and went on to be a salesman. The big, tall, dark-haired, blue-eyed man was everyone's friend.

In January 1920, Prohibition began. It was a time when the government passed a law making alcohol illegal. Unfortunately, this law produced many jobs for criminals. Kelly was one. He became a "society bootlegger" in Memphis, Tennessee, selling people liquor. Kelly, however, was not all that smart, and was soon caught and run out of town. He continued bootlegging, spending time in and out of jail. In 1927, he met a young woman who changed his life forever.

Born in 1904 and named Cleo, the pretty dark-haired girl lived in Saltilo, Mississippi with her parents, James and Ora Brooks. She loved to dream and often imagined herself a rich and powerful princess — the opposite of her real life. Her family was painfully poor. Soon her mother deserted her father, and Cleo went with her mother. Now she didn't even have a whole family.

Cleo was not yet in her teens when she met Lonnie Fry. They were married, had a daughter, and divorced by the time Cleo was 14. These were difficult years for the young girl.

Cleo went to live with her mother in Texas. She hated her name, and at the age of 15 changed it to the more romantic "Kathryn." By 1921, Kathryn was in the bootlegging business. She'd bring the booze to her mother's hotel, where it would be sold. Mother and daughter made enough money to live on.

While working, Kathryn met another bootlegger, Charlie Thorne. They were married in 1924. It was a rough and wild marriage that ended one night three years later.

Kathryn stopped to fill her car up at the gas station. Angrily, she waited impatiently for the attendant to fill her tank. "Hey, Kate, what's the matter?" asked the man.

"I'm bound for Coleman to kill that Charlie Thorne," replied Kathryn coldly as she paid the man. Without another word, she pushed the gas pedal to the floor and blasted down the road, headed for Coleman, Texas.

The attendant shook his head. He knew this couple. They were always fighting. This time, though, Kate looked mad enough to follow through on her threat. Still, it was none of his business. They'd probably make up.

The following day Charlie Thorne was found dead, a bullet in his head. Beside him was a note: "I can't live with her or without her, hence I am departing this life." Although his death was judged a suicide, many believe it was Kathryn's doing.

It was this dangerous woman who later that year met yet another bootlegger. This man, she thought, could *be* something. And so began Kathryn's transformation of the not-too-smart, good-old-boy George, into the FBI's Most Wanted: "Machine Gun" Kelly.

CHAPTER 2 — A GIFT

George Kelly didn't like guns, but he liked his booze, often drinking away much of his profits and supplies. He wasn't a tough guy, although he pretended to be. The big man had a nasty, growling voice, which he copied from gangsters he had met. It was this man who impressed the pretty Kathryn by snarling, "No copper will ever take me alive."

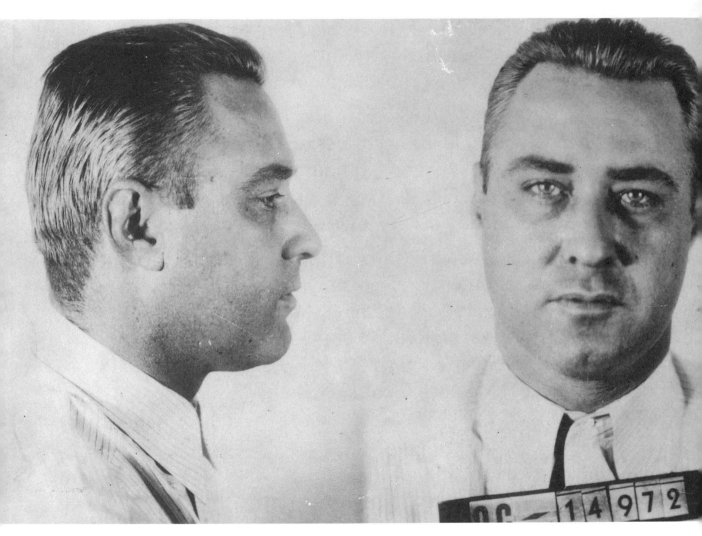

"Machine Gun" Kellys' mug-shot.

Kelly's fake stories of big bank robberies and underworld dealings made him great in the young 23-year-old's eyes. Perhaps he could give her the power and money she had wanted all her life. Kathryn came to love the big man, but she soon realized his big-time tales were all lies.

Still, Kathryn had plans for Kelly. By this time, her mother had married a man by the name of Robert G. "Boss" Shannon. Together, the Shannons were running a "fugitive farm" for criminals in Paradise, Texas. Here, for $50 a night, hoodlums could hide out from the police for as long as they needed to, or could pay. At the Shannon Ranch, Kathryn introduced Kelly to many gangsters, but the big man didn't have the experience to work with them. He had to prove himself, and Kathryn set about finding a way for him to do just that.

"But, Kate, I don't even like guns," whined a hung-over Kelly. He had never shot a gun or even hurt anyone in his whole life.

"But you've got to be able to hurt people," argued the determined Kathryn. "You've got to be tough or nobody will respect you. You gotta have the respect, George. And I know something that will get you the respect."

With that Kathryn went shopping. On her return, she presented Kelly with a gift — a gleaming, new machine gun.

"Uh, thanks, Kate," said George upon opening the gift. He was caught in a trap. Kathryn wasn't going to let him continue to be the happy, drunken, pretend-gangster he had been all these years. She was going to make him start working for real.

"Now you have to practice," said Kathryn.

She led him out to the fence on the Shannon Ranch. The young woman placed walnuts along the top rail. "Shoot them off," said Kathryn.

Kelly tried. He didn't even come close. Each shot made him jump, and for a man with a "bum ticker," it was quite a toll on his heart. "Keep practicing," said Kathryn, undaunted.

Kelly had no choice. It took months before he could shoot the walnuts off the fence, but eventually Kelly proved himself to be an excellent marksman. Now Kathryn had to get him in with the "right people."

CHAPTER 3 —

KATHRYN'S "MACHINE GUN" HUSBAND

While Kelly remained at the ranch, Kathryn drove to nearby Fort Worth, Texas. She hit all the big "speakeasies" — places where illegal liquor was sold. She always found gangsters who were willing to listen to a pretty girl, and Kathryn took the chance to rave about her man, the "big time" bank robber.

With a handful of Kelly's .45-caliber cartridges, Kathryn approached her "friends." "Here's a souvenir I brought you," she whispered. "It's a cartridge fired by George's machine gun — Machine Gun Kelly, you know."

"Where is this great sharpshooter?" asked one criminal, turning the cartridge over in his hand.

"He's away robbing banks," lied Kathryn. In fact, Kelly was usually home getting drunk or sleeping off a hangover. Although he had mastered his machine gun he still hadn't pulled off any jobs, nor did he really want to. He was just a bootlegger, although his name, "Machine Gun" Kelly, was becoming widely known throughout the criminal underworld.

Speakeasies' were a favorite hangout for gangsters.

In 1930, Kelly was arrested by Prohibition agents while driving a truckload of whiskey. Kelly surrendered without a fight. He was convicted and sentenced to one year in Leavenworth Federal Prison in Kansas.

While Kelly spent his time in the "Big House," Kathryn continued to build her easy-going husband's reputation into that of a hardened criminal. " 'Machine Gun' is in Kentucky robbing banks," she lied.

By now, even Kelly was beginning to believe the stories Kathryn told about him. In prison, he started telling a few of his own tales.

"This place is getting on my nerves, Red," said Kelly in his toughest gangster voice to a fellow prisoner, safecracker Morris "Red" Rudensky. "I've got 50 grand sitting on the outside, and I could throw a party that would last a year. But I can't get at it."

"Why don't you go over the wall?" asked Rudensky, impressed.

Escaping wasn't what Kelly had in mind. He might get killed! Thinking fast, he quickly replied, "I'm

"Machine Gun" Kelly in Leavenworth Prison.

16

too old for that, Red. I'll be out in a year. But if you get any ideas, I'll help you for laughs. You young guys are the ones who should be licking your chops over busting out. And if you do, you might help old George make his wheels spin a little faster."

"Old George" was all of 34 by the time he left Leavenworth Prison in 1931. Returning to the Shannon Ranch, he and Kathryn were married. Kathryn insisted he practice up with his machine gun. Her husband was going to be a successful bank robber, even if she had to push him all the way.

"Look at these newspaper articles," said Kathryn, pointing to clippings on the kitchen table. "The Barrows and the Barkers and Pretty Boy Floyd are making all the headlines. They're getting away with big-time hauls. We can do it, too." With that, Kathryn got her husband a job with a local gang. Reluctantly, George hit the bank-robbing trail.

Leavenworth Prison housed some of America's most notorious criminals.

CHAPTER 4 — KELLY TURNS KIDNAPPER

Together with his gang of small-time robbers, Kelly hit several banks in Mississippi and Texas. As luck would have it, the mean-sounding, tough criminal with a machine gun never had to prove himself. All the bank jobs went smoothly — Kelly never had to fire at anyone.

Still, Kelly's reputation grew. Back home in Texas, Kathryn overheard someone say, "A guard was blown away on the Wilmer bank robbery by Machine Gun Kelly." Kelly hadn't killed anyone, but Kathryn now believed she had made him into a big-timer. She was proud of her man and of herself. However, for all his successful jobs, Kelly wasn't bringing home much money. The early 1930s was a time of the Great Depression. People had no money to save. The small-town banks that Kelly was hitting hardly made him enough to live off of. Kathryn began thinking and planning again.

"George, look at these," she said.

Stumbling over to the table, Kelly peered down at the newspaper clippings with hung-over eyes. This time his wife wasn't looking at stories on bank robberies.

The drought of the early 1930s left the southwestern United States in a virtual dustbowl.

"Look at this," said Kathryn, holding up one article. "William Hamm, Jr. was kidnapped and held for $100,000 ransom. We've got to put the snatch on one of these birds, George. It's the only way to make any money these days."

Kelly looked skeptical. "Too risky," he said.

"We're going to do it, George," said Kathryn in her determined voice.

George gave in. He'd go along with whatever Kathryn thought up. Nodding his head meekly, the tough-as-nails Machine Gun Kelly turned to look for a drink.

CHAPTER 5 — THE JOB

An Indiana businessman was the couple's first choice. However, Kathryn herself ruined this plan.

"We're going to make a fortune off this guy," said a drunken Kathryn to two Fort Worth detectives sitting in a local speakeasy. Believing them to be crooked, the 29-year-old schemer spilled the entire plan.

Ed Weatherford and J.W. Swinney took the information and headed right for the police station. By the next day, the businessman's home was circled with security guards. There was no kidnapping him. The funny thing was that the man was broke anyway! He had nothing, and the kidnapping couple wouldn't have gotten any money for him. Perhaps it was luck or fate, but Kathryn had to pick a new target.

Their next victim was much better off. Charles F. Urschel was a millionaire oilman living in Oklahoma City. Kathryn was sure they could get a cool $200,000 off him. Teaming up with an old friend, con man and swindler Albert Bates, Kelly approached the Urschel home on the night of July 22, 1933.

Except for not knowing which one of the two men on the porch was Urschel, the job went flawlessly. Tied and blindfolded, Urschel was driven to the Shannon Ranch, where the next part of Kathryn's complex plan unfolded.

On July 26, a package was sent to Mr. J.G. Catlett, a close friend of Urschel's who lived in Tulsa, Oklahoma. The package contained three typewritten letters: one to Urschel's wife, a second to Catlett, which instructed him to take the third letter to another friend, Mr. E.E. Kirkpatrick in Oklahoma City. Kirkpatrick's letter had the ransom demands:

> "Immediately upon receipt of this letter you will proceed to obtain the sum of TWO HUNDRED THOUSAND DOLLARS ($200,000.00) in GENUINE USED FEDERAL RESERVE CURRENCY in the denomination of TWENTY DOLLAR ($20.00) Bills.

> "It will be useless for you to attempt taking notes of SERIAL NUMBERS, MAKING UP DUMMY PACKAGE, OR ANYTHING ELSE IN THE LINE OF ATTEMPTED DOUBLE CROSS. BEAR THIS IN MIND, CHARLES F. URSCHEL WILL REMAIN IN OUR

CUSTODY UNTIL MONEY HAS BEEN INSPECTED AND EXCHANGED AND FURTHERMORE WILL BE AT THE SCENE OF CONTACT FOR PAY-OFF AND IF THERE SHOULD BE ANY ATTEMPT AT ANY DOUBLE XX IT WILL BE HE THAT SUFFERS THE CONSEQUENCE."

Kirkpatrick was also instructed to run an ad in the *Daily Oklahoman* Newspaper, where a P.O. Box was listed. On July 28, a letter arrived in the box, postmarked from Joplin, Missouri. It read:

"...You will pack TWO HUNDRED THOUSAND DOLLARS ($200,000.00) in USED GENUINE FEDERAL RESERVE NOTES OF TWENTY DOLLAR DENOMINATION in a suitable LIGHT COLORED LEATHER BAG and have someone purchase transportation for you, including berth, aboard Train #28 (The Sooner) which departs at 10:10 p.m. via the M.K.&T. Lines for Kansas City, Mo.

"You will ride on the OBSERVATION PLATFORM where you may be observed by some-one at some Station along the Line between Okla. City and K.C. Mo. If indication are alright, some-where along the Right-of-Way you will observe a Fire on the Right Side of Track (Facing direction train is bound) that first Fire will be your Cue to be prepared to throw BAG to Track immediately after passing SECOND FIRE.

"REMEMBER THIS — IF ANY TRICKERY IS ATTEMPTED YOU WILL FIND THE REMAINS OF URSCHEL AND INSTEAD OF JOY THERE WILL BE DOUBLE GRIEF — FOR, SOME-ONE VERY NEAR AND DEAR TO THE URSCHEL FAMILY IS UNDER CONSTANT SURVEILLANCE AND WILL LIKE-WISE SUFFER FOR *YOUR ERROR.*"

"If there is the slightest HITCH in these PLANS for any reason what-so-ever, not your fault, you will proceed on into Kansas City, Mo. and register at the Muehlebach Hotel under the name of E.E. Kincaid of Little Rock, Arkansas and await further instructions there.

"THE MAIN THING IS DO NOT DIVULGE THE CONTENTS OF THIS LETTER TO ANY LAW AUTHORITIES *FOR WE HAVE NO INTENTION OF FURTHER COMMUNICATION.*

YOU ARE TO MAKE THIS TRIP
SATURDAY JULY 29TH 1933..."

Unbeknownst to the Kellys, Mrs. Urschel had immediately called the FBI minutes after her husband was kidnapped. They were following the entire case. However, the FBI's first concern was for the safe return of Mr. Urschel. Although every letter was reviewed by the Feds, they instructed Mrs. Urschel and Kirkpatrick to follow through on the demands. However, contrary to instructions, serial numbers were recorded on all the $20 bills.

On the night of July 29, 1933, Kirkpatrick boarded the designated train and walked up to the observation platform. Miles away, Kelly and gang got into their car, preparing to drive to the rendezvous points and light the signal fires. Nervously, Kelly turned the key. The car didn't start. He pushed the gas pedal.

"What's wrong?" asked Kathryn impatiently.

"It won't start." replied Kelly. By this time, he had flooded the engine. Eventually, they got the car going. They arrived at the first signal fire just in time to watch the train, and their $200,000, race by. Kathryn's complicated scheme was ruined. They had to go to Plan B.

On Sunday, July 30, in his hotel room, Kirkpatrick received a telegram:

> "Owing to unavoidable incident unable to keep appointment. Will phone you about six. Signed C.H. Moore." (Kelly used Moore as an alias.)

That evening, Kelly gave Kirkpatrick new instructions. Half an hour later, Kirkpatrick walked down Linwood Avenue in Kansas City, holding tightly to the bag containing $200,000. A tall, heavyset man stepped from a nearby car and walked along beside him.

"I'll take that bag." whispered Kelly nervously.

"How do I know you're the right man?" asked Kirkpatrick coolly, studying Kelly's appearance and clothes.

"You know I am," said Kelly angrily.

"I want some instructions," demanded Kirkpatrick. "Two hundred thousand dollars is a lot of money. I want some kind of assurance that Mr. Urschel will not be harmed."

"Don't argue with me!" growled Kelly. "The boys are waiting." Actually, only Albert Bates sat in the nearby car.

27

"I want a definite answer I can give to Mrs. Urschel. When will her husband be home?" demanded Kirkpatrick.

"He'll be home in 12 hours," said Kelly, nervously shifting his weight from foot to foot.

Kirkpatrick dropped the bag to the sidewalk and walked away. Grabbing it, Kelly raced for the car. The money was his!

CHAPTER 6 — FREED AND CAPTURED

"We have to kill him," argued Kathryn. "We've got the money, now let's get rid of this old man. With no witnesses, no one is going to identify us."

"No," said Kelly stubbornly. "It's bad for future business. How are we ever going to get anyone to pay off on another job if they know we'll just kill the guy anyway?"

"Kill him," said Kathryn.

"He's going free," said Kelly, standing up to his wife for the first time. It was a noble gesture, and his ultimate undoing.

Released on the outskirts of Oklahoma City with $10 for a cab, Charles Urschel arrived home at

11:30 p.m., July 31, almost exactly nine days to the minute from when he was abducted.

After several hours of sleep, he met with FBI agents. Urschel's memory was amazing. He remembered times, people, places. Although he had been blindfolded virtually the entire time, he had kept track of voices and smells. Soon, the FBI tracked down the location of the Shannon Ranch and picked up Kathryn's mother and husband. Shortly thereafter, on August 12, 1933, Albert Bates was picked up in Denver, Colorado.

As for Kathryn and Kelly, they headed north into Minnesota and Illinois, freely spending the ransom money every chance they got. However, upon learning of the Shannons' capture, Kelly was enraged. He wrote several letters to Urschel and to other government officials and witnesses, threatening to kill them if the Shannons were convicted. However, his fierce confidence was shattered when Bates was picked up. Turning to Kathryn, he said, "It's all over!"

Investigations into Kelly's whereabouts continued. Several $20 bills were traced down into Memphis, Tennessee. There, on September 26, 1933, FBI agents from Birmingham, Alabama, together with local Memphis Police, burst in on the couple's room.

Police Sergeant W.J. Raney was the first to break through the door. Pointing his gun directly into Kelly's large stomach, he stated fiercely, "George Kelly, you are under arrest."

Calmly, almost as if he was glad it was finally over, Kelly replied quietly, "I've been waiting for you."

EPILOGUE

Kelly, Kathryn, Bates, and the Shannons were all convicted, receiving life sentences.

The rough, tough Machine Gun Kelly was sent to maximum security prison on Alcatraz. He grew back into the mild-mannered man he really was, gaining a new nickname: "Pop Gun" Kelly.

Eventually, Kelly was transferred to Leavenworth Prison in Kansas. In 1954, Kelly wrote a letter to his old victim, Charles Urschel, stating: "These five words seem written in fire on the walls of my cell: Nothing can be worth this!" He learned his lesson too late, for later that year, on July 17, Kelly died of a heart attack. He never walked as a free man after that last fateful day in September 1933. His glorious reputation and big-time kidnapping job had cost him everything.

Four years later, Kathryn was released from prison. Her once-famous husband now dead, her youth, dreams, and wealth gone, she faded away into society, just another ex-criminal who had served her time.

Alcatraz Island, maximum security prison.